Strength
IS THE ENERGY OF
God!

Also by Della Reese-Lett

Angels Along the Way:
My Life with Help from Above

Coming Home

God Inside of Me

What is This Thing Called Love?

THE REVEREND

Della Reese

Strength

IS THE ENERGY OF

God!

HAMPTON ROADS
PUBLISHING COMPANY, INC.

For information write:

Hampton Roads Publishing Company, Inc.
1125 Stoney Ridge Road
Charlottesville, VA 22902

Or call: 804-296-2772
Fax: 804-296-5096
e-mail: hrpc@hrpub.com
www.hrpub.com

If you are unable to order this book from your local
bookseller, you may order directly from the publisher.
Call 1-800-766-8009, toll-free.
Library of Congress Catalog Card Number: 00-111872
ISBN 1-57174-269-7
10 9 8 7 6 5 4 3 2 1
Printed on acid-free paper in Canada

We tend to forget, which was the first sin. We forgot who we were. We must take it literally that we are made in the image-likeness of God, and therefore, all the qualities of God are in us. All that God is, *I am*. And so are you. All that God has is mine, and yours too. But we have to have the strength of this knowledge. I think these thirty-one days will make you more consciously aware, and therefore, stronger.

In Strength,
The Reverend Della Reese-Lett

Strength

IS THE ENERGY OF

God!

Day One

"In the
beginning
God . . ."

Genesis 1:1

All strength
originates in Spirit. . . .
and God is Spirit.

Because I am made in the image-likeness of God, I *am* strong, and I have the capacity to accomplish any endeavor.

Day Two

> "The name (nature)
> of the LORD is a
> strong tower:
> the righteous run
> into it and are safe."
>
> Proverbs 18:10

*Righteousness is right thinking followed
by right actions, which are right words,
right feelings, and right reactions.*

I affirm the strength of God in all
situations, circumstances, and conditions.

Day Three

"Because of His strength will I wait upon Thee: for God is my defense."

Psalms 59:9

"No" is a good word.

Because of the strength of my character
(the Christ in me), I *am* able to say
"no" at the appropriate time.

Day Four

"... but my
Father who lives
in me does His
work through
me."

John 14:10

*Because of Jesus' awareness of his divinity
and his relationship to God, he was able
to accomplish all that he set out to do,
teaching us how to do the same.*

I know that only God is real . . . only
good is real and goodness is in me,
expressing through me.

Day Five

> "... be strong in the LORD, and in the power of His might."
>
> Ephesians 6:10

When things are not going well, remember you have the strength of God to stand your ground.

The strength of God in me is so strong it cannot be defeated!

Day Six

"I can do all things
through Christ
which
strengtheneth me."

Philippians 4:13

STRENGTH is . . . knowing *that it is the
God in you that enables you to do what you do.*

My mental strength allows me
to hold to the thought that
the LORD is my strength.

Day Seven

"Wait on the LORD: be of good courage, and He shall strengthen thine heart: wait, I say, on the LORD."

Psalms 27:14

Be patient.
God will handle it.
God will strengthen you.

I stand still. I let go. I let God,
and I see the salvation of the Lord.

Day Eight

"Be strong and of
good courage. . . ."

Joshua 1:6

Courage is a spiritual quality that
enables us to be and remain poised.

In the midst of any and all challenges,
circumstances, situations, and conditions I
am poised and centered in God.

Day Nine

"I am the vine, you are
the branches. He
who abides in Me,
and I in him bears
much Fruit . . ."

John 15:5

God, Almighty and Universal, is a
Spiritual Presence constantly striving
to express in and through us.

Because I have great strength of cause,
I move toward the fulfillment of
God's plan for me. And the goodness
in me expresses through me.

Day Ten

"Cast all your anxieties on Him, for He cares about you."

I Peter 5:7

Strength is balance.

Real STRENGTH enables me
to maintain balance in my life,
world, and affairs.

Day Eleven

"We then that are
strong ought to
bear the infirmities
of the weak. . . ."

Romans 15:1

*Helping others always brings new
and magnificent experiences.*

The strength in my heart reaches out
in Unconditional Love, knowing
there is a piece of God in everybody.

Day Twelve

"Eye has not seen,
nor ear heard, nor
has entered into the
heart of man the
things which God has
prepared for those
who love Him."

I Corinthians 2:9

*My strength is knowing He loves me and
I love Him, so I am assured by His word
He will never leave me or forsake me.*

I wait on the LORD . . . and
He strengthens my heart.

Day Thirteen

"Then God blessed them, and God said to them, 'Be fruitful and multiply; fill the earth and subdue it; have dominion over the fish of the sea, over the birds of the air and over every living thing that moves on the earth.'"

Genesis 1:28

All that we have and ever will have comes from God. We do not earn it. It is ours by right of inheritance.

He is the Gift and the Giver.

Day Fourteen

> ". . . freely ye
> have received;
> freely give."
>
> Matthew 10:8

Giving is the first step to receiving.
It is the working of the law.

I have the strength (of God) to work
the Law of Giving and Receiving.

Day Fifteen

"For God has
not given us a
spirit of fear,
but of power
and of love . . ."

II Timothy 1:7

*You have the strength to stay
focused on your divine path.*

I walk the walk of Christ,
I talk the talk of Christ.
I live the Christ.

Day Sixteen

"Do not be anxious
about anything, but
in everything, by
prayer and petition,
with thanksgiving,
present your
requests to God . . ."

Philippians 4:6

*You need strength to withstand
any pressures of anxiety.*

I am not anxious about anything because
I have the strength of God to wait.

Day Seventeen

"Fear not, for I AM with
you; be not dismayed,
for I AM your God.
I will strengthen you,
Yes I will help you.
I will uphold you with My
righteous right hand."

Isaiah 41:10

*God is your protector in all
conditions, circumstances,
situations, and challenges.*

I stand still and see the saving
grace of the LORD, my God.

Day Eighteen

"Finally . . .
whatsoever things are
true, whatsoever things
are noble, whatsoever
things are just, . . .
whatsoever things
are pure, . . . whatsoever
things are of good report
. . . meditate on these.

Philippians 4:8

I cannot afford a negative attitude.
Negative attitudes come from
a disbelief in the word of God.

Because I have a personal relationship
with God, I go forward in peace.

Day Nineteen

"For the Spirit
searches all things,
yes the deep things
of God."

I Corinthians 2:10

You need strength to know that God
will never leave you nor forsake you;
and that God will reveal to you
what you need to know,
when you need to know it.

Whatever I need to know,
whenever I need to know it,
all is revealed to me.
Thank you, God.

Day Twenty

"But Thou art holy,
O Thou that
inhabitest the
praises of Israel."

Psalms 22:3

*Praising God is something you
feel and know in your heart
and speak with your words.*

God is my salvation.

Day Twenty-One

"The LORD is the strength of my life; of whom shall I be afraid?"

Psalms 27:1

I am not afraid, for God is my deliverance.

God is my continuous saving grace and
will always, in all ways, deliver me.

Day Twenty-Two

"So God created
man in his image,
in the image of God
created He him;
male and female
created He them."

Genesis 1:27

*You have the strength of the Spirit of
God to stand up to any challenge.*

I am wonderfully and magnificently made.

Day Twenty-Three

"For great is Your
mercy toward me,
and You have
delivered my soul
from the depths
of the grave."

Psalms 86:13

Strength is inner, deep.
It is like still water.

The unlimited strength of God
in me surfaces just in time,
in just time.

Day Twenty-Four

"And God is
able to provide you
with every blessing
in abundance . . ."

II Corinthians 9:8

". . . it is our Father's
good pleasure to
give you the
kingdom."

Luke 12:32

*Because Jesus knew His purpose, He
was able to get to it and get through it.*

Because Jesus shows me the way,
I can meet any and all challenges
through the Christ in me.

Day Twenty-Five

"But I say unto you,
that you resist
not evil. . . ."

Matthew 5:39

*Because Jesus worked His principles
of love and non-resistance in the
midst of trials and turmoil, He
was able to hold His peace.*

I will fear no thing or no one,
for greater is God in me than
anything or anyone in this world.

Day Twenty-Six

> ". . . all the days
> of my appointed
> time will I wait,
> till my change
> come."
>
> Job 14:14

*You have to open your mind and
allow for life's changes, or you just keep
getting the same beating all the time.*

Strength is the ability to see
clearly through any change.
I welcome the new gifts from God.

Day Twenty-Seven

"Jesus said
to him, 'Rise,
take up your bed
and walk.'"

John 5:8

In order to make my overcoming,
I must pick up my bed and walk.

By using God-principles I can rise from the
ashes of any challenge, circumstance, or
situation to new good in my life.
Thank you, God.

Day Twenty-Eight

">. . . according to
the eternal purpose
which He
accomplished in
Christ Jesus
our Lord."

Ephesians 3:11

*In order to accomplish our purpose,
we need to use God's principles
which can give us the strength
to do what we have to do.*

True strength is of God; and
God's peace and grace is amazing.

Day Twenty-Nine

> ". . . the God of all
> grace . . . will
> Himself restore,
> establish, and
> strengthen you."
>
> 1 Peter 5:10

*Because a part of us is human, we must
strengthen that part so that the
spiritual part of us can do its work.*

Because God is never going to come
down to me, I must step up to God . . .
And *I am* glad about that.

Day Thirty

"I press toward
the mark for the
prize of the high
calling of God in
Christ Jesus."

Philippians 3:14

You have the strength to
change your mind, and raise
your thoughts to a high holy place.

By readjusting my thoughts and feelings, I
can endure, through my strength,
whatever I need to.

Day Thirty-One

"Be strong and of good courage, do not fear nor be afraid of them; for the LORD your God, He is the One who goes with you. He will not leave you nor forsake you."

Deuteronomy 31:6

God Almighty is a spiritual presence evenly present, ever ready to fill us with new courage and a fearlessness beyond description . . .

I fear no evil for Thou art with me.
Knowing this I will not resist, for
what I resist persists. My spirituality
is my power to release stress.

Strength Is the Energy of God is one of a planned twelve-book series, one book for each month, dedicated to providing daily reminders of God's greatest gifts.

In 1987 Della Reese-Lett was ordained as a minister by the Universal Foundation For Better Living, an organization of twenty-two churches and study groups worldwide founded by the Reverend Doctor Johnnie Colemon. Della had been teaching a class at her home in order to further the Principles that she had found so useful in her own life. What began with eight people around her dining room table has grown into Understanding Principles for Better Living Church (UP), which now has a weekly attendance of more than three hundred. Reverend Della's message of practical Christianity has been an inspiration to so many and the church is growing so rapidly that a new facility is needed and plans are underway for UP's new church home. The church maintains a web page at www.upchurch.org.

Scriptural References

Scripture taken from the New King James Version, Nashville: Thomas Nelson, Inc., 1982 and Holy Bible, New Living Translation, Wheaton, Ill.: Tyndale House Publishers, Inc., 1996.

Photo Credits

Day	Photographer	Day	Photographer
1	Virginia C. Colburn	17	Rebecca M. Parrish
2	Virginia C. Colburn	18	George Durr
3	George Durr	19	George Durr
4	Virginia C. Colburn	20	Richard F. Ashley
5	Richard F.Ashley	21	Judalon Smyth
6	George Durr	22	Richard F. Ashley
7	Rebecca M. Parrish	23	George Durr
8	Judalon Smyth	24	Judalon Smyth
9	Richard F. Ashley	25	George Durr
10	George Durr	26	George Durr
11	George Durr	27	Virginia C. Colburn
12	Virginia C. Colburn	28	George Durr
13	Virginia C. Colburn	29	Richard F. Ashley
14	George Durr	30	Rebecca M. Parrish
15	Rebecca M. Parrish	31	Richard F. Ashley
16	George Durr		

Hampton Roads Publishing Company

. . . for the evolving human spirit

Hampton Roads Publishing Company
publishes books on a variety of subjects,
including metaphysics, health, integrative medicine,
visionary fiction, and other related topics.

For a copy of our latest catalog, call toll-free
(800) 766-8009, or send your name and address to:

Hampton Roads Publishing Company, Inc.
1125 Stoney Ridge Road
Charlottesville, VA 22902

e-mail: hrpc@hrpub.com
www.hrpub.com